THE COMPUTER AGE

BY CHRIS OXLADE

WHAT IS A COMPUTER?

Today, computers are everywhere, doing all sorts of different jobs — helping people to write letters, acting as games machines, controlling robots and even flying planes. But how can a computer do all these different things? The answer is that it is a general-purpose electronic machine controlled by a computer program. Change the program and the job that the computer does changes, too. A computer stores and processes different types of information (called data), such as numbers, letters, pictures and sounds. The same computer can be a calculator, games machine or word processor, just by selecting the right program. All computers work like this, from personal computers at home to super-powerful scientific computers.

WHAT IF... COMPUTERS HAD NEVER BEEN INVENTED?

People who use computers today would still be doing their jobs on paper, with pens and pencils, typewriters and calculators. Finding information that is stored on computers, including train times and telephone numbers, would take longer. Many science and engineering problems would never have been worked out, because computers were needed to do the complex calculations to solve them.

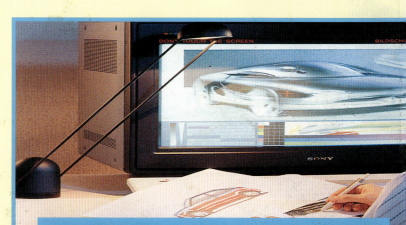

COMPUTERS AT WORK

Business computers do all sorts of office jobs, such as word processing, accounting, storing customer details, ordering goods and so on. Computers are also used for design work, such as book, magazine and advert design (above), engineering design and video production.

HARDWARE & SOFTWARE

Computers are made up of hardware and software. The hardware is the physical parts of a computer – its microchips, cables, screen, keyboard, mouse and so on. Software is the programs and data that a computer uses. It is often loaded onto the computer from CD-ROMs or the Internet.

TRAINING SIMULATIONS

Some computers are programmed for just one job. This one acts as a flight simulator. It recreates the movements of a Boeing 747 airliner, as well as the sound of the engines and the view from the windows. Pilots use the simulator to train to fly new types of aircraft, and to help them deal with emergency situations, such as engine failure.

COMPUTERS AT HOME

If you have a computer at home, what do you use it for? Perhaps it's for playing games, writing projects for school, looking up information on an encyclopedia CD-ROM or surfing the Internet. Other members of your family might also use it for writing letters, making greetings cards, or keeping their bank accounts up to date.

CALCULATING MACHINES

n the 1940s, computers were developed that work in the same way as those we use today. However, the history of the computer dates back long before then, starting with its forerunner, the calculator, designed to help with sums. The first calculator was the abacus, which originated in Asia about 5,000 years ago, and is still used today in classrooms and shops in some areas of the world. The abacus is really an aid to adding rather than a machine that calculates. The first real calculating machines were mechanical, but they could do only simple additions and subtractions. Developed at the same time as these calculating machines were manufacturing machines controlled by punched cards. These were important in the development of computers because changing the pattern of holes in cards changed the way that the machine worked. So the machines were programmable in a similar way to modern computers.

EARLY CALCULATING MACHINES

The first calculators were people, who worked things out in their heads, or counted on their fingers and toes. Then came counter-casting, where people moved counters on a special board to aid calculation. Early abacuses, such as those used in ancient Rome and Greece, had pebbles in grooves. Later abacuses had beads on wires, as this picture of a Chinese abacus shows. With practice, simple sums can be performed almost as quickly on an abacus as they can on an electronic calculator.

PROGRAMMED PATTERNS

The first programmable machine was the Jacquard loom, which was invented in 1804 by Frenchman Joseph-Marie Jacquard. The pattern woven by the loom was controlled by cards with holes punched in them. Changing the pattern of holes changed the pattern woven into the cloth.

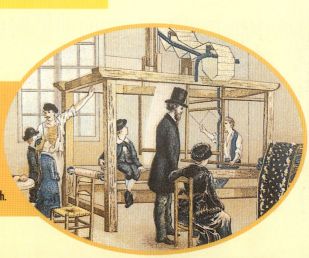

PASCAL'S CALCULATOR

One of the first machines capable of adding and subtracting automatically was built by the French scientist and mathematician Blaise Pascal in 1642. It worked using a series of toothed wheels which turned one another. The first wheel represented units, the second tens, and so on.

COMPUTER PIONEER

Charles Babbage (1791–1871) was an English mathematician and inventor. He is remembered as the person who first developed the idea of the digital computer (see page 6). Babbage was Professor of Mathematics at Cambridge University, and was also responsible for developing the postal system in England.

BEADS FOR NUMBERS

The modern abacus consists of a wooden frame holding wires along which beads slide. On a Chinese abacus, the bottom beads count one and the top beads count five. Moving a bead to the centre bar makes it part of the sum. In the photograph, the number 61 is represented. The illustration (right) shows how the first column counts units, the second tens, the third hundreds, and so on. Once all the beads at the bottom of a column are at the centre bar, the number is carried over to the top bar, and so on from column to column.

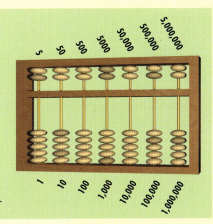

MECHANICAL COMPUTER

The machine here is called a Difference Engine. It was built from plans drawn by Charles Babbage. It automatically calculates mathematical tables. Babbage also designed an Analytical Engine, never built because of its great complexity and expense. This machine would have been programmed by punched cards to do complex calculations. It would have had a calculating section, a memory section and inputs and outputs, much like a modern electronic computer.

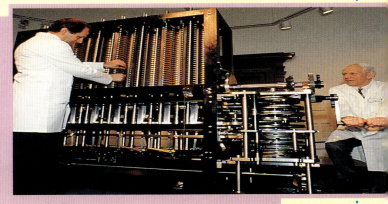

THE FIRST COMPUTERS

The next stage in the history of computers was the development of machines that could do a whole series of calculations automatically. These computers used instructions from a program, rather than just adding or subtracting numbers entered manually. Numbers were represented digitally by combinations of open and closed switches. The first machines like this were electromechanical, using electromagnetic switches which were turned on and off by electric currents. The switches controlled other currents, which in turn controlled other switches. Complex circuits of switches could perform simple sums. The next stage was the arrival of electronic computers in which switches were replaced by electronic devices called vacuum tubes. These devices had no moving parts and so could work hundreds of times faster, carrying out thousands of sums every second.

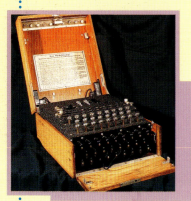

SOLVING AN ENIGMA

Shown here is an Enigma coding machine used by Germany, Italy and Japan during the Second World War to encode top-secret messages before they were transmitted. One of the first electronic computers, called Colossus, was built secretly in England in 1943 to decipher the Enigma codes.

ENIAC

One of the most important steps in the development of computers was the completion of ENIAC (Electronic Numerical Integrator and Computer) at the University of Pennsylvania in 1946. This was the first electronic computer that could be programmed to do almost any sort of calculation. It could do 5,000 additions per second.

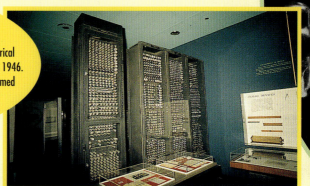

MONSTER MACHINES vs MONSTER POWER

Early computers were huge. ENIAC (see above) measured 2.5 metres (8 ft) high and 24 metres (78 ft) long, and contained some 18,000 vacuum tubes. Six thousand modern notebook computers (left), each thousands of times more powerful than ENIAC, would fit into the same space.

PROBLEM-SOLVING

Most early computers, such as the Merlin at Brookhaven National Laboratory, New York (seen here), were built by scientists to carry out complex mathematical calculations needed for their work. The Merlin had a 32,000-word memory, and could do 100,000 additions per second and 20,000 multiplications per second.

COMPUTERS FOR SALE

Computers were first developed in the 1940s for scientific and military purposes. Business computers such as the UNIVAC (Universal Automatic Computer) appeared in the 1950s. They were very large and expensive, and less powerful than a modern home computer. Personal computers, known as PCs for short, first appeared in the 1970s.

VACUUM TUBES

The main electronic parts of early computers were called vacuum tubes, or simply valves, because they controlled the flow of electricity. These bulb-like components, shown here being made, contained parts that had to glow red-hot to work. Air was pumped from the glass tube to stop the parts burning up. Vacuum tubes did the same job as modern transistors and diodes, but were thousands of time larger.

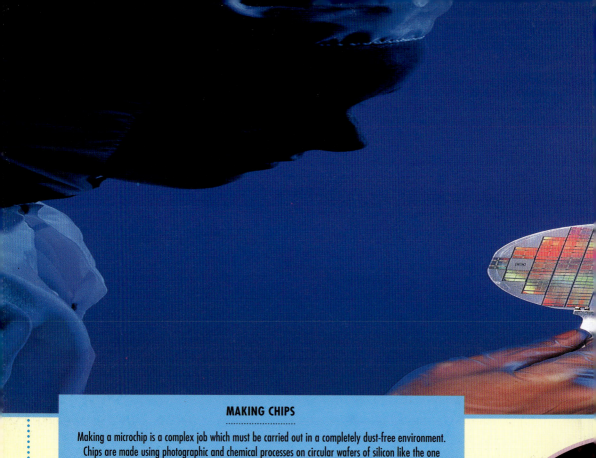

MAKING CHIPS

Making a microchip is a complex job which must be carried out in a completely dust-free environment. Chips are made using photographic and chemical processes on circular wafers of silicon like the one shown here. Each wafer contains several individual chips, which are broken off and then tested.

CHIP PROTECTION

This picture shows a microchip soldered to a circuit board. What you see is the protective ceramic case in which the chip itself is encapsulated. The wire 'legs' carry electricity in and out of the chip. The tracks on the board carry an electric current between the chips and other components.

Wire legs

Microchip case

Circuit board

Tracks

ELECTRONIC SWITCHES

A single transistor has three connections. The strength of the electric current flowing between two of the connections is controlled by the current which flows to the third connection. So a small current can turn a large current on and off. Transistors are made of materials called semiconductors.

Computers using vacuum tubes, such as ENIAC, are often called first-generation computers. In 1947, the first prototype transistor was invented at the Bell laboratories in the USA. The transistor acts as an electronic switch and, once it was perfected in the late 1950s, it quickly replaced the vacuum tube in computers. Transistors are small and reliable, and use far less electricity than vacuum tubes. Transistor-based computers, often called second-generation computers, were smaller, faster and cheaper than first-generation computers. The next major development of electronics came in the late 1960s, with the integrated circuit. This enabled thousands of transistors and other electronic components to be built onto a tiny chip of silicon. Computers using these silicon chips or 'microchips' were faster and smaller still, and are classed as third-generation computers.

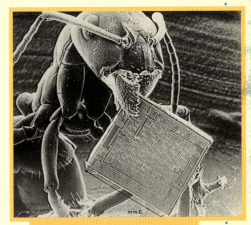

CLEVER COMPONENTS

This single microchip, held in the jaws of an ant, contains thousands of components. Inside a computer, all but a few of the electronic components are built onto chips. All the tiny components and the connections between them are built up by adding layers of different materials. Each chip or collection of chips has its own job to do, such as remembering data, or helping to control a disk drive.

CHIPS IN SPACE

The computers on board the *Apollo* spacecraft, which carried astronauts to the Moon, were designed in the 1960s. They had less power than a modern scientific calculator, but were state-of-the art machines at the time. The computers helped the astronauts to navigate to the Moon and back, and to land on the Moon.

D uring the 1960s and 1970s, computers became both powerful and cheap enough for companies to buy them for their businesses. For example, banks bought them for storing information about their customers' accounts and for updating their details quickly and efficiently. In 1971, the first example of a new type of microchip, called the microprocessor, appeared. This made it possible to build a small computer with a microprocessor and a few other components. Soon, the first 'microcomputers', or personal computers, such as the Commodore PET and APPLE II were available. In the early 1980s, small computers for use at home were developed, which introduced millions of people to computer programming. Computers that use microprocessors are known as fourth-generation computers.

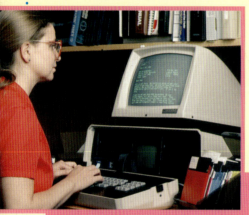

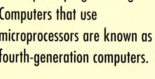

NOT SO PORTABLE

Compared to today's notebook computers, early portable personal computers were extremely cumbersome and heavy. The Osborne computer, seen here, had a removable lid with keyboard, a tiny built-in screen and disk drives. It could also be plugged into an external monitor.

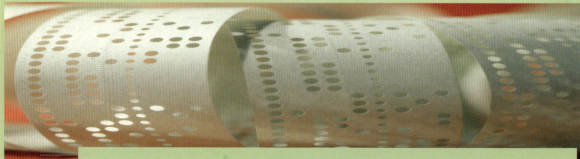

INFORMATION ON PAPER

The first business computers had no keyboards for entering data directly and no monitors for seeing it. Instead, a separate keyboard created patterns of holes in paper tape, which was called punched tape. Each row of holes across the tape represented a digit or character. The tape was then fed into a reading device in the computer.

TAPE STORAGE

Modern computers have large internal memories and disk drives to store data. Older machines, such as the one shown here, had small internal memories and stored their data on large, removable spools of magnetic tape. Data was read from a tape, processed by the computer and stored on another tape.

THE ZX80

In 1980, Sinclair Research in Britain launched the ZX80, the first computer designed for hobbyists to use at home. It had a Zilog Z80 microprocessor, 1 kilobyte of memory and its output was displayed on a domestic television. Programs were written in a programming language called BASIC and stored on a separate cassette tape recorder.

OFFICE JOBS

In the early 1970s, all business computers were either mainframe computers (see page 12) or less powerful minicomputers, such as the popular PDP-8 shown above. They were used for data processing, such as working out salaries, stock control or accounts. Many of these jobs, and more, are now done by desktop computers.

THE FIRST MICROCOMPUTERS

The Apple II was one of the first desktop computers designed for office use. The computer itself was contained in a small case which included a keyboard and supported a black-and-white monitor. Data was stored on floppy disks which slotted into its disk drives.

MODERN COMPUTERS

What do you think of when you visualize a computer? You probably picture the type of computer you have at home or at school. This is called a personal computer, or PC. It is normally a desktop machine, consisting of a case containing the computer itself, a monitor (screen), a keyboard and a mouse, and is designed to be used by just one person. Most people use this type of computer, both in the office and at home. The other types include mainframe computers and supercomputers. Mainframes are used by large companies for data processing (for example, in banking, insurance, and by airlines for booking tickets and boarding passengers). These computers are powerful enough to be used by many people at the same time from individual terminals. Supercomputers are designed to do complex calculations extremely quickly.

IN THE PICTURE

This animator is using a workstation, a small computer much more powerful than a standard personal computer. Workstations are used for jobs that need complex calculations to be done very quickly, such as drawing highly detailed three-dimensional graphics, or scientific calculations.

PARALLEL PROCESSING

Supercomputers, such as the Cray-2, are the most powerful computers of all. They are designed to perform calculations at extremely high speed. The fastest can manage hundreds of billions of calculations every second. In a supercomputer, calculations are carried out by many different processors working together. This is called parallel processing.

PORTABLE COMPUTERS

A palm-top computer is a cross between a personal computer and an electronic organizer. Palm-tops are not as powerful as standard personal computers, but can run simple programs, such as word processors, and can send and receive electronic mail (E-mail). A notebook computer is a personal computer contained in a folding case about the size of a piece of A4 paper and only a few centimetres thick.

PERSONAL COMPUTERS

The original personal computer was developed by IBM in the early 1980s. In offices, PCs are mostly used for word processing, accounting and other similar work. At home, PCs can do similar jobs, but normally have additional parts, such as speakers, which make them suitable for playing games and using other leisure-type software.

THE MACINTOSH

Most personal computers are known as PCs. They used to be called IBM-compatible PCs, because their software was compatible with the first IBM personal computer. The other main type of personal computer is the Apple Macintosh or Mac. The Mac was the first computer to have what is known as a desktop-type screen with icons (small images that stand for items such as discs and programs). Macs are popular with people who work in the media, such as book designers and video editors.

INSIDE A PC

If you could see inside a computer, you would see dozens of electronic parts, mechanical parts and wires linking everything together. A computer is a complicated machine, but it's easier to understand if you think of it as being made up of simpler sections. The main parts inside a computer (the hardware) are described below. The other important hardware items found outside the computer, such as monitors, printers and keyboards, are often described as peripherals. You can read about them on pages 18-19.

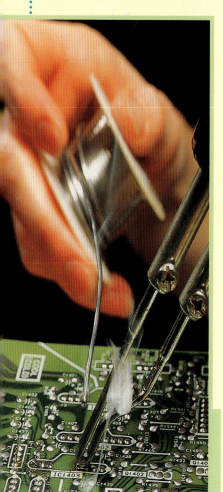

HARD DRIVE

Most personal computers have a hard disk drive built into the case. This stores a large amount of data in the computer itself, additional to the memory chips.

CIRCUIT BOARDS

The computer's circuit boards, such as its motherboard, are made from plastic. Microchips and other components have metal legs which slot into holes in the board and are soldered into place. Metal tracks on both sides of the board connect the components together to make electrical circuits.

MEMORY BANKS

Memory chips are electronic data stores. There are two types of memory. The data in random access memory (RAM) can be changed, but is lost when the electricity supply to the computer is turned off. The data in read-only memory (ROM) cannot be changed, but is permanent. The size of a computer's memory is measured in kilobytes (K) and megabytes (MB).

MOTHER & DAUGHTER

A major component of a personal computer is the circuit board, known as the motherboard. It contains the microprocessor, the memory chips and connections for other parts, such as the monitor, keyboard and disk drives. Other smaller circuit boards, called daughterboards, plug into the motherboard. They might control graphics or sound. Plug-in boards like the one shown here make the repairing or upgrading of components very easy.

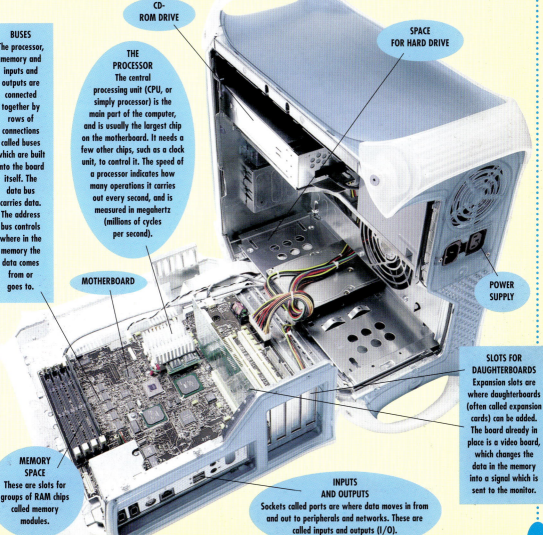

CD-ROM DRIVE

SPACE FOR HARD DRIVE

BUSES
The processor, memory and inputs and outputs are connected together by rows of connections called buses which are built into the board itself. The data bus carries data. The address bus controls where in the memory the data comes from or goes to.

THE PROCESSOR
The central processing unit (CPU, or simply processor) is the main part of the computer, and is usually the largest chip on the motherboard. It needs a few other chips, such as a clock unit, to control it. The speed of a processor indicates how many operations it carries out every second, and is measured in megahertz (millions of cycles per second).

MOTHERBOARD

POWER SUPPLY

SLOTS FOR DAUGHTERBOARDS
Expansion slots are where daughterboards (often called expansion cards) can be added. The board already in place is a video board, which changes the data in the memory into a signal which is sent to the monitor.

MEMORY SPACE
These are slots for groups of RAM chips called memory modules.

INPUTS AND OUTPUTS
Sockets called ports are where data moves in from and out to peripherals and networks. These are called inputs and outputs (I/O).

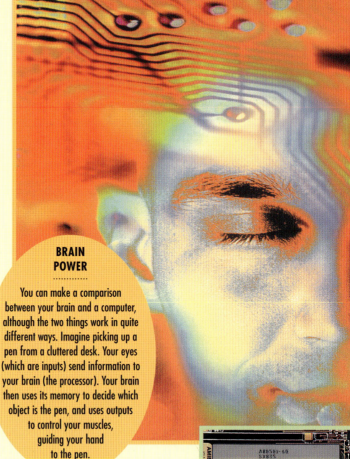

SIMPLE LOGIC

A processor uses electronic circuits called logic gates to do calculations and other jobs. Each gate does a simple operation, but groups of gates connected together can do more complex operations, such as adding.

For example, a NOT gate has an input and an output. When there is a 1 at the input, there is a 0 at the output, and when there is a 0 at the input, there is a 1 at the output.

Here are symbols and truth tables for a NOT gate and an OR gate.

NOT GATE

in	out
0	1
1	0

OR GATE

inputs		output
A	B	
0	0	0
0	1	1
1	0	1
1	1	1

What about this combination of gates, called a NOR gate? Can you complete the table by working out what should go in the output column?

NOR GATE

inputs		output
A	B	
0	0	
0	1	
1	0	
1	1	

Answer on page 32.

BRAIN POWER

You can make a comparison between your brain and a computer, although the two things work in quite different ways. Imagine picking up a pen from a cluttered desk. Your eyes (which are inputs) send information to your brain (the processor). Your brain then uses its memory to decide which object is the pen, and uses outputs to control your muscles, guiding your hand to the pen.

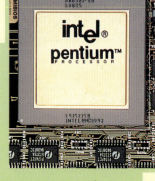

INSIDE THE PROCESSOR

The processor is made up of two parts. The arithmetic unit carries out calculations and other operations on data. The control unit receives instructions from the program, collects data, tells the arithmetic unit what to do with it, and stores data back in memory. The processor also has some memory inside, where it stores results of calculations temporarily.

MICROSOFT MAN

Bill Gates (1955-) is the man who founded Microsoft, the company that created the operating system MS-DOS and Windows. These programs are now used on almost every PC in the world. Gates left university early to start Microsoft with a friend, and became a billionaire in 1986 when the company was floated on the stock market.

T he two main parts of a computer are its central processing unit (CPU), or processor for short, and its memory. The processor is the computer's brain. In a personal computer, the CPU is a microprocessor. The CPU takes data from memory or inputs, processes it in some way and then sends it to memory or outputs. A program, which is a list of instructions (also stored in memory) tells the CPU what to do. Software needs to be loaded into memory before it can be used, normally from disk drives where it is stored permanently. Software is divided into system software and application software. You can find out more about applications on page 24. Some system software is stored in the computer's read-only memory (ROM) for instant use.

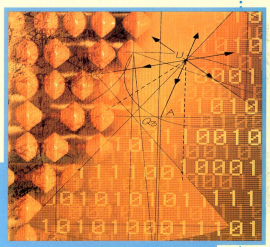

SYSTEM SOFTWARE

System software tells a computer how to do routine jobs, such as looking to see what keys have been pressed on the keyboard, or which way the mouse is moving, or getting data from the hard disk drive. Today, the majority of PCs use system software called MS-DOS and Microsoft Windows.

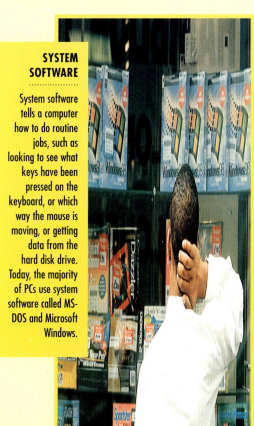

INFORMATION IN BITS

Computers store information as binary numbers. Binary is a counting system which uses just the digits 0 and 1. These digits can easily be represented in electronic circuits by turning currents on and off. Each 0 or 1 stored is called a bit. Almost any sort of information can be stored using binary numbers. This table shows how a row of eight bits (called a byte) represents the decimal number 65.

Decimal	128	64	32	16	8	4	2	1
Binary	0	1	0	0	0	0	0	1

Binary numbers also represent words, pictures, video pictures and sounds, using standardized codes. For example, when you see the letter 'A' on your screen, it is represented in memory by the binary number 01000001, in a code called ASCII.

PERIPHERALS

A computer that cannot communicate with the outside world is useless. It needs to be able to receive data through its inputs to process and send out data through its outputs. There are many different devices that plug into computers, and these are collectively called peripherals. Some, such as scanners, are input devices. Others, such as printers, are output devices. Some, such as hard disk drives, are both input and output devices. Peripherals are connected to the computer using electronic circuits called interfaces. Most interfaces, such as SCSI and USB, are standard, which means that you can plug any device into the same slot in the computer. Mainframe and supercomputers also have peripherals such as printers, but they are normally bigger and faster than those used for personal computers.

GAMES PLAYING

A joystick is an input device designed for playing games. It detects which way the player is pushing it and also has one or two 'firing' buttons.

COMPUTER PHOTOGRAPHY

There are two ways of storing a photograph on a computer. The first is to use a digital camera, which has a special light-sensitive silicon chip instead of the film found in a normal camera. Photographs are stored in the camera's memory before being downloaded (sent) to the computer. The second way is to copy printed photographs into the computer using a peripheral called a scanner.

PEN BUT NO PAPER

Most data, such as words and numbers, is entered into a computer on a keyboard. But computers still use pens, too. A light pen is an input device that can be used to select choices on a computer screen simply by touching the screen with the pen. The pen has a light sensor at its tip that detects the scanning spot of light on the screen, and software works out where the pen is pointing. Pens are also used to draw on graphics tablets, which are electronic drawing boards.

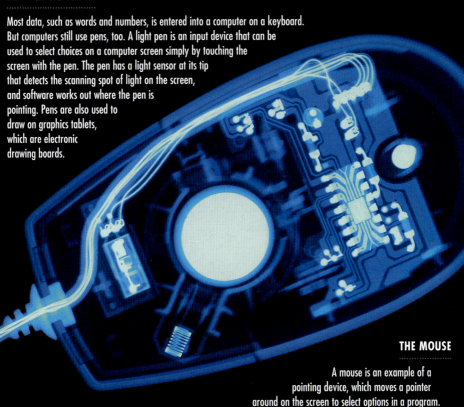

THE MOUSE

A mouse is an example of a pointing device, which moves a pointer around on the screen to select options in a program.

EXTERNAL STORAGE

There are several different devices that store software (programs and data). Magnetic disk drives (of either the hard or floppy type) store binary numbers as magnetic patterns on a plastic disc covered in magnetic material. Compact disc (CD) and digital versatile disc (DVD) drives store binary numbers as tiny pits on a plastic disc which are changed and read by laser.

MAKING A COPY

A printer makes a copy of data on paper. The most common for home use is the ink-jet printer, which makes patterns of colour by firing tiny dots of ink onto the paper. In a laser printer, the images are made by toner melted onto the paper. The pattern of toner is controlled by a small laser fired at the paper.

VIRTUAL WORLDS

A virtual world is a world created using computer graphics and sound. A virtual-reality headset has two small screens inside, one for each eye, which show a stereo image of the world, and headphones which play stereo sound. This tricks the person wearing the headset into thinking that he or she is really in the particular world being created.

100%

500%

1000%

PIXELS

On a computer screen, all images are made up of hundreds of rows of tiny squares called pixels. The colour that each pixel appears on the screen is set by a number in the computer's video memory. Scanned images and painted images are stored pixel by pixel in memory or on disk.

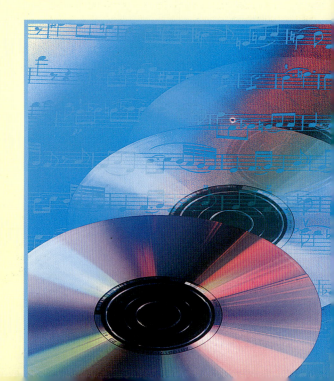

Anything that appears on a computer screen that is not simple text is called a graphic. Graphics make computer programs easier to use, and are important for design, engineering and games. Two-dimensional (2D) graphics are images which look flat on the screen, such as icons (small images on the screen that stand for items, such as disks and programs), photographs and word-processor pages. Some 2D images, such as photographs, are made up of thousands of tiny coloured squares. Others, such as plans and drawings, are made up of lines and shapes. Computers can also draw three-dimensional graphics.

Any images and sounds that are stored in binary on a computer are described as digital. They can be stored, manipulated and transferred between computers.

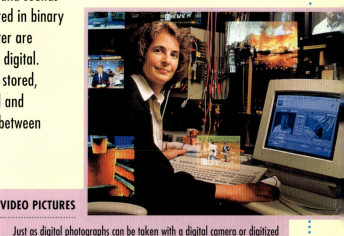

VIDEO PICTURES

Just as digital photographs can be taken with a digital camera or digitized from normal photographs with a scanner, digital video can be taken with a digital video camera or digitized from television or tape using special equipment. The video can then be viewed or edited on-screen.

SOUND IN BITS

Sound is stored on computer and on music CDs in digital form. With a suitable program, digital sound can be played and edited on computer. Some electronic keyboards can be connected to a personal computer, allowing music played on the keyboard to be edited and replayed by the computer.

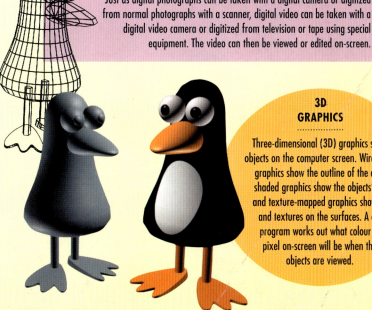

3D GRAPHICS

Three-dimensional (3D) graphics show objects on the computer screen. Wire-frame graphics show the outline of the objects, shaded graphics show the objects' surfaces, and texture-mapped graphics show patterns and textures on the surfaces. A complex program works out what colour each pixel on-screen will be when the objects are viewed.

NETWORKS

If you have used the Internet, your computer has been part of a network. A network is simply a group of computers linking together so that they can share data and programs, printers, disk drives and so on. For example, in an office, one computer might store data about customers. Everyone in the office can access information stored on the server (the main computer) from their own computer. A network can consist of just two computers in the same room, dozens of computers in the same building, or thousands of computers in a large organization. The Internet is a huge network of computers spread right around the world. Anyone can be part of it by connecting their computer to a telephone line. It allows people to send messages (E-mails) to anyone else who is connected, and to look at information stored on other computers.

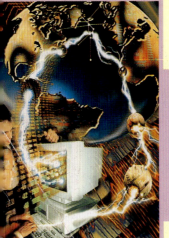

TELEPHONE LINKS

A set of computers spread over a large area, normally linked together using telephone lines, is called a wide-area network (WAN). If telephone lines are used, the computers connected to them need a modem. When you are connected to the Internet, you are part of a wide-area network that covers the whole world.

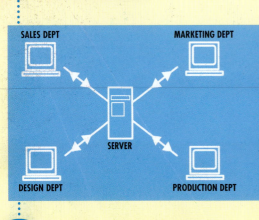

SALES DEPT   MARKETING DEPT

SERVER

DESIGN DEPT   PRODUCTION DEPT

SMALL NETWORKS

A local-area networ (LAN) is a collection of computer and peripherals in the sam office or building connecte together by wires. Each machine needs special software and hardware to connect it to the network. Local-area networks often have a fast computer with a very large set of disk drives called a server that the other computers use.

REMOTE ACCESS

Users of portable computers (notebooks and palm-tops) can connect to computers at their homes or offices simply by plugging into the telephone network or by using a mobile phone. This is called remote access. It's useful for people on the move for sending and collecting E-mails.

MODEMS

The word 'modem' stands for modulator/demodulator. It turns computer data into signals which can travel along the telephone line, and turns signals on the telephone line from other computers back into computer data.

THE WORLD WIDE WEB

People connected to the Internet can create information on their machines which other Internet users can look at. This system is called the World Wide Web (WWW). Each set of information is called a web site. There are millions of web sites around the world, run by organizations, companies and individuals.

COMPUTER APPLICATIONS

With the right program, a computer can do almost any job. Each different job is called an application, and the programs that make a computer do the jobs are called application programs. Most personal computers have a basic set of application programs, such as a word processor, spreadsheet, database and web browser (for looking at information on the World Wide Web). Specialist applications include desktop-publishing programs, computer-aided design programs, three-dimensional drawing programs and video editing software. At home, you may use applications such as games and educational programs, photograph editing programs, or garden design programs, as well as a simple word processor and address book. In industry, personal computers and mainframe computers have applications specially written for their own jobs.

TEXT ON SCREEN

With a desktop-publishing system you can mix text from a word processor with photographs and other images to create a complete book. The screen shows what the finished pages will look like. A book printer can use the data from the program to print the finished books.

STANDARD APPLICATIONS

Most computers, especially office computers, are used for a few similar jobs, such as writing letters and reports, storing information, or doing calculations. Most of these jobs can be done with just three application programs, examples of which are shown right. Other common applications are web browsers, E-mail, desktop publishing and presentation programs.

Word processor – for writing and editing text
eg. Word for Windows and Word 98

Spreadsheet – for doing calculations
eg. Excel and Lotus

AIDS TO DESIGN

Using a computer to design objects is called computer-aided design (CAD). This car designer can see exactly what the car he is designing will look like from any angle. He can make as many changes to the design as he likes before the real thing is made. Architects also use CAD, and can use virtual reality to 'walk' through the buildings they are designing.

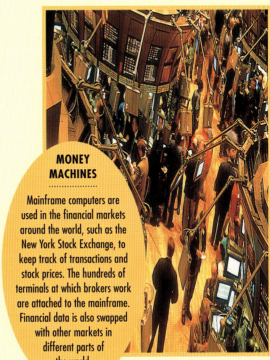

MONEY MACHINES

Mainframe computers are used in the financial markets around the world, such as the New York Stock Exchange, to keep track of transactions and stock prices. The hundreds of terminals at which brokers work are attached to the mainframe. Financial data is also swapped with other markets in different parts of the world.

LOOKING GOOD

Presentation software is used to help make presentations in business or in schools, taking the place of projector slides. It can show pages of text, graphs, pictures and video in the order that the presenter wants. The presentation is shown on the computer's screen, or on an overhead projector using a special transparent screen.

Database – for storing and looking up information eg. Oracle and Access

DESIGN YOUR OWN COMPUTER GAME

Computers are controlled by a list of instructions called a program. Programs must be written in a language that the computer understands, such as BASIC, C or FORTRAN. Finished programs have to be thoroughly tested, and any mistakes (called bugs) removed. Before you type a program into a computer, you must work out exactly what it's going to do. Below you can find out how to do this first step for a simple computer game.

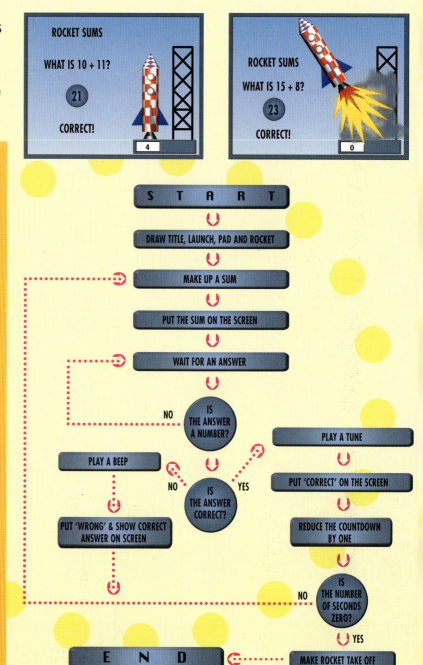

ROCKET SUMS

WHAT IS 10 + 11?

21

CORRECT!

4

ROCKET SUMS

WHAT IS 15 + 8?

23

CORRECT!

0

1 THE GAME IDEA

Start by working out an idea for the game. Here's an idea for a simple adding game:

ROCKET SUMS
- Player must work out answers to simple sums shown on screen.
- Picture of a rocket in corner of screen.
- Time until take off written on launch pad under rocket.
- If player answers correctly, time is reduced by one and tune plays.
- If player answers incorrectly, time stays the same, beep noise plays and correct answer is displayed on screen.
- When countdown reaches zero, rocket takes off across screen, filling screen with stars, and game ends.

2 WHAT IT LOOKS LIKE

Now make some sketches of what the screen or screens of your game will look like. Some examples for the adding game are shown at the top of this page. Think about the text, sound and animations you want to use.

3 DRAW A FLOW DIAGRAM

Now draw a flow diagram of the program, using the example shown right as a guide. Each step of the program has its own box in the diagram, and arrows show how the steps follow each other. Computer programmers try to divide the program into easy sections. Many sections are repeated lots of times as the program runs, and they only need to be written once.

START

DRAW TITLE, LAUNCH, PAD AND ROCKET

MAKE UP A SUM

PUT THE SUM ON THE SCREEN

WAIT FOR AN ANSWER

IS THE ANSWER A NUMBER? — NO

PLAY A TUNE

PLAY A BEEP

IS THE ANSWER CORRECT? — NO / YES

PUT 'CORRECT' ON THE SCREEN

PUT 'WRONG' & SHOW CORRECT ANSWER ON SCREEN

REDUCE THE COUNTDOWN BY ONE

IS THE NUMBER OF SECONDS ZERO? — NO / YES

MAKE ROCKET TAKE OFF

END

If you have surfed the Internet, you will have seen plenty of web pages. These on-screen pages provide information about all kinds of people, companies and organizations, including schools. They are called 'multimedia' pages because they contain text, photographs, diagrams, video clips, sound and music to display information.

Try designing some web pages on paper as part of an Internet site for your school. Think about what information could be in the form of pictures, video and sound. For example, there could be a page of photographs of all the teachers, and a recording of the school song.

Start with a 'home' contents page which would lead the user to the other pages. Use the pictures below to give you some ideas.

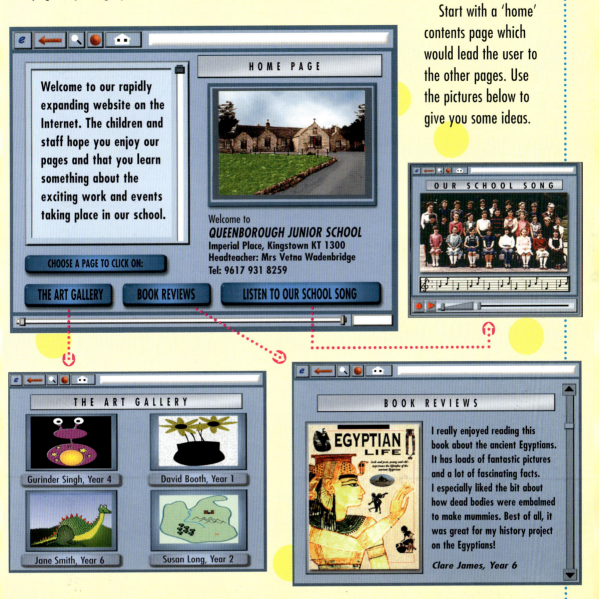

HOME PAGE

Welcome to our rapidly expanding website on the Internet. The children and staff hope you enjoy our pages and that you learn something about the exciting work and events taking place in our school.

Welcome to
QUEENBOROUGH JUNIOR SCHOOL
Imperial Place, Kingstown KT 1300
Headteacher: Mrs Vetna Wadenbridge
Tel: 9617 931 8259

CHOOSE A PAGE TO CLICK ON:

THE ART GALLERY   **BOOK REVIEWS**   **LISTEN TO OUR SCHOOL SONG**

OUR SCHOOL SONG

THE ART GALLERY

Gurinder Singh, Year 4

David Booth, Year 1

Jane Smith, Year 6

Susan Long, Year 2

BOOK REVIEWS

EGYPTIAN LIFE

I really enjoyed reading this book about the ancient Egyptians. It has loads of fantastic pictures and a lot of fascinating facts. I especially liked the bit about how dead bodies were embalmed to make mummies. Best of all, it was great for my history project on the Egyptians!

Clare James, Year 6

ENVIRONMENTAL CONTROL

Computers have a part to play in controlling and improving our environment. The treatment of sewage, for example, is often carried out in computerized wastewater treatment plants like the one shown here. In some buildings, conditions are monitored and adjusted by computer. Many modern skyscrapers have sensors around the building to measure temperature, humidity and so on, and to control the air conditioning. The telephone and firefighting systems, and even the lifts, are also computerized.

IN-CAR COMPUTERS

Specialized computers in cars are becoming increasingly common. Large cars have computerized engine management, which ensures that the engine is working efficiently all the time. Formula 1 racing cars have on-board computers which send data about each car back to the pits, where engineers can spot any problems. Navigation computers have an electronic map which tells the driver where he or she is all the time.

FLYING COMPUTERS

Modern fighter aircraft would be impossible for a pilot to fly without the help of a computer. The pilot controls where the aircraft goes, but the computer actually does the flying because it can react much more quickly than the pilot. A computer also controls the fighter's radars and weapons.

SPECIALIZED COMPUTERS

When is a computer invisible? When hidden away inside another machine. The job of many computers is to operate a machine, such as a washing machine, automatically. Some of these computers are standard machines with special application software. Others need no keyboards, screens or disk drives, but are made up of just a microprocessor and some memory containing a program. These computers have inputs and outputs connecting them to other parts of the machine. For example, in a microprocessor-controlled washing machine, a sensor in the drum detects the water depth and sends data to the microprocessor. The microprocessor is connected to the inlet valve, which it opens to let water into the drum.

COMPUTER WORKERS

Inside many factories, computers control the manufacturing process, constantly checking that everything is working efficiently. Industrial robots are also computer controlled. Machines such as drills and lathes can be connected to computers so that they cut out the parts that an engineer has designed on the computer. This is called computer-aided manufacture (CAM).

GAMES MACHINE

A games console is a computer dedicated to creating animated three-dimensional graphics. They have powerful processors and special graphics chips. They don't need parts that normal computers have, such as keyboards, mice and printers.

CHANGING ROLES

Today, computers are a very common sight. We are used to having them in schools, at home and in offices. But even in the mid 1970s, when personal computers were first introduced, only people in the computer departments of companies had ever seen a computer. An office worker of the 1950s might not recognize an office of today. Then, instead of word processors and printers, there were dozens of typewriters and typists to operate them, and instead of databases, there were huge filing cabinets full of paper. Since then, computers have had an effect in most areas of our lives, such as making work, communications and transport more efficient. But not all of the effects have benefitted everyone. In some cases, people have lost their jobs because computers are doing the work instead. And some people argue that children should be playing outdoors or reading books instead of playing computers games.

EXCHANGING ROLES

If you made a telephone call in the nineteenth century, you had to tell a telephone operator who you wanted to speak to. The operator connected the two telephones by plugging in wires. Mechanical automatic exchanges were introduced in the early twentieth century, but telephone operators were still needed. In a modern electronic telephone exchange, millions of telephone calls, fax messages, E-mails and computer data messages are routed from one telephone to another completely automatically by computers. The computers also keep track of who is making the calls and produce the customers' bills. Computer programmers and engineers are needed to maintain the exchange.

SHOPS ON-LINE

With a computer and Internet connection, you can buy things 'on-line' without leaving home. On-line shopping is great for people who are too busy, or who find it difficult to get to the shops. But it's unlikely that on-line shopping will replace trips to the high-street shops.

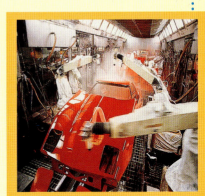

MAKE IT EASY

Spot the difference between a modern car plant and a car plant of the 1950s. Robots, controlled by computers, have taken the place of many of the workers. The robots work happily 24 hours a day, 7 days a week, and never get bored!

COMPUTER LESSONS

It's important to know how to use a computer, so computer studies are now a subject at school. Computers also help children with writing and studying other subjects.

GLOSSARY

Byte
A 'word' of data, normally made up of eight binary digits.
A kilobyte (K) = 1,024 bytes; a megabyte (MB) = 1,024 K.

Data
Information stored in and processed by a computer.

Input
Where data goes into a computer.

Microcomputer
A small desktop computer, normally with a single processor. Most personal computers
are microcomputers.

Minicomputer
A medium-sized computer used for data processing in offices.

Output
Where data comes out of a computer.

Personal computer (PC)
A small desktop computer normally used by just one person. The term 'PC' can mean any sort of personal computer,
but is normally used to mean an IBM-compatible personal computer (the sort that works with Microsoft Windows).

Supercomputer
An extremely fast and powerful computer designed for carrying out complex scientific calculations.
Supercomputers are the most powerful computers of all.

Answer for page 16.

The completed table for a NOR gate looks like this:

inputs		out-put
A	B	
0	0	1
0	1	0
1	0	0
1	1	0

The idea or 'logic' of this is easier to understand if you think of it in terms of a real situation. For example, imagine if the output was your decision as to whether or not to wear a jumper. This would depend on two factors or outputs, such as whether it was hot, and whether you were going running. You could draw up a table like the one shown right and compare it to the NOR gate table.

Inputs		Output
Is it hot?	Are you going running?	Will you wear a jumper?
No	No	Yes
No	Yes	No
Yes	No	No
Yes	Yes	No

ACKNOWLEDGEMENTS

We would like to thank David Rooney and Elizabeth Wiggans for their assistance. Artwork by John Alston.
Copyright © 2000 ticktock Publishing Ltd.
First published in Great Britain by ticktock Publishing Ltd., The Offices in the Square, Hadlow, Tonbridge, Kent TN11 0DD, Great Britain.
All rights reserved. No part of this publication may be reproduced, stored in a retrieval system, or transmitted in any form or by any means electronic,
mechanical, photocopying, recording or otherwise, without prior written permission of the copyright owner.
A CIP catalogue record for this book is available from the British Library. ISBN 1 86007 112 0 (paperback). 1 86007 163 5 (hardback).

Picture research by Image Select. Printed in Hong Kong.

Picture Credits: t = top, b = bottom, c = centre, l = left, r = right, OFC = outside front cover, OBC = outside back cover, IFC = inside front cover

Ann Ronan @ ISI; 6c. Apple Computer UK Ltd; 6bl, 12/13 (main pic) & OFC (main pic), 15b. Corbis; 4/5t, 6/7c, 8/9c, 10cl, 10b, 10/11t, 11br,
12tl, 30/31t & OFC (inset), 31cr. Deutsche Telekom; 28cl. FPG International; 7cr. ISI; 2/3b, 6/7t, 10/11c, 11c, 12bl, 16cr, 18cl, 18bl, 18/19b,
22/23b. Mary Evans Picture Library; 4cl, 4br, 5tr, 5ct, 5br. PIX; 16/17t & IFC, 20/21b. Rex Features; 9cr, 16bl, 17bl. Science Photo Library; 6cl,
21cr. Telegraph Colour Library; 2cl, 3br, 8cb & OBC, 8cb, 13tl, 20t & OFC, 20/21t, 23br, 25cr, 30cl. Tony Stone; 2/3t & 32, 3tr, 8/9t, 9br, 12br,
14l, 14cr, 14cb, 17cr, 18/19 (main pic), 22cl, 22/23t, 24cl, 24/25t, 25br, 28bl, 28/29t, 28/29c, 29br, 30b, 31tr, 31b.

snapping-turtle guide

Every effort has been made to trace the copyright holders and we apologize in advance for any unintentional omissions.
We would be pleased to insert the appropriate acknowledgement in any subsequent edition of this publication.